yukibooks.com/b/d6d046

baby

bebé

boy

niño

friends

amigos

girl

niña

smile

sonreír

cry

llorar

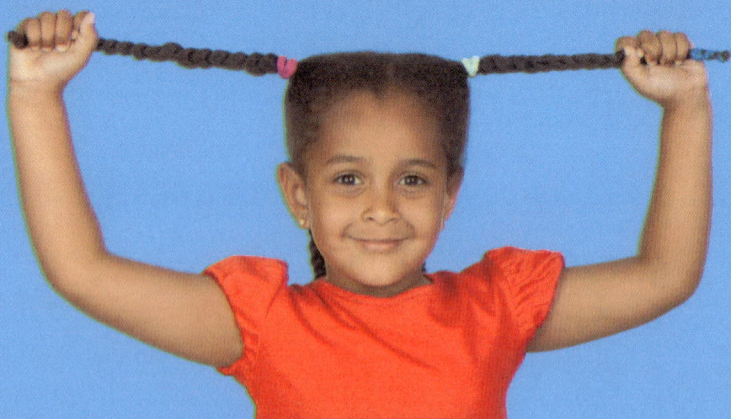

hair

cabello

eye

ojo

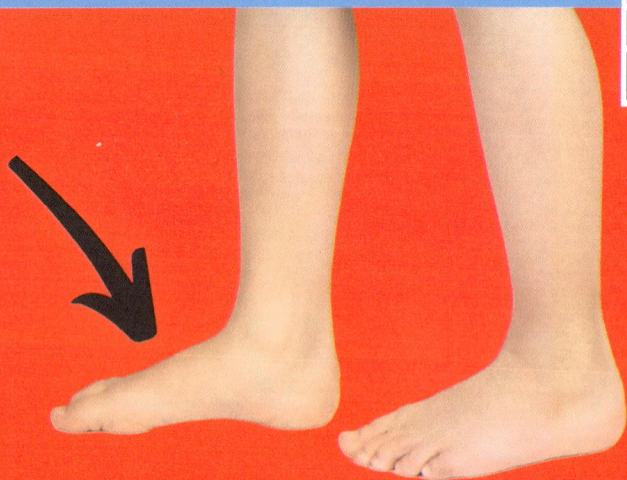

foot

pie

hand

mano

nose

nariz

teeth

dientes

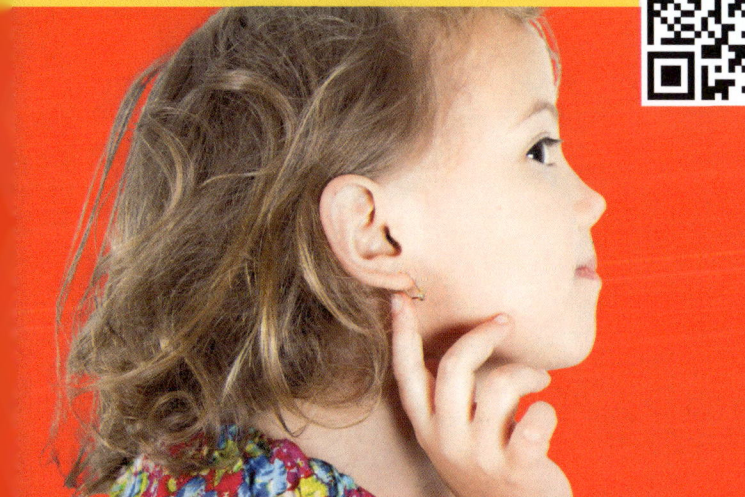

ear

oreja

tongue

lengua

sun

sol

moon

luna

star

estrella

tree

árbol

bird

pájaro

coat

abrigo

pants

pantalones

dress

vestido

shoes

zapatos

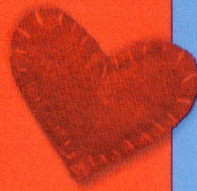

red

rojo

blue

azul

yellow

amarillo

pink

rosa

white

blanco

green

verde

black

negro

multicolored

multicolor

rainbow

arcoíris

apple

manzana

banana

plátano

tomato

tomate

orange

naranja

carrot

zanahoria

peas

guisantes

potato

patata

corn

maíz

lemon

limón

grapes

uvas

pear

pera

watermelon

sandía

zucchini

calabacín

egg

huevo

mushroom

seta

square

cuadrado

circle

círculo

rectangle

rectángulo

triangle

triángulo

cat

gato

dog

perro

fish

pez

cow

vaca

duck

pato

chick

pollito

hen

gallina

frog

rana

pig

cerdo

rabbit

conejo

mouse

ratón

horse

caballo

sheep

oveja

flower

flor

butterfly

mariposa

ladybug

mariquita

snail

caracol

cake

pastel

bread

pan

clock

reloj

key

llave

book

libro

ball

pelota

table

mesa

plate

plato

chair

silla

high chair

trona

fork

tenedor

knife

cuchillo

spoon

cuchara

cup

taza

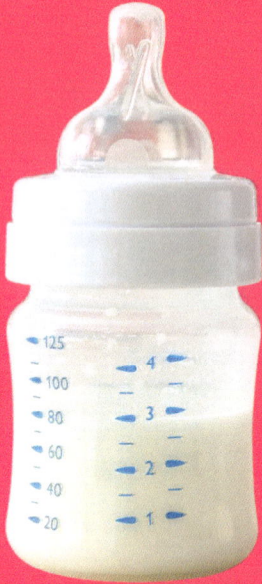

baby bottle

biberón

glass

vaso

bed

cama

crib

cuna

teddy bear

oso de peluche

pacifier

chupete

towel

toalla

sink

lavabo

toothbrush

cepillo de dientes

soap

jabón

toilets

inodoros

potty

orinal

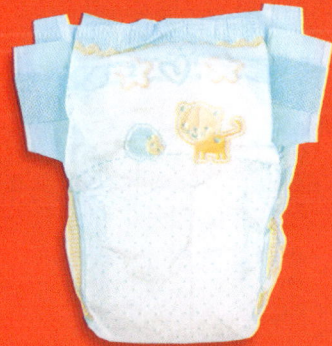

diaper

pañal

car

coche

bike

bicicleta

plane

avión

boat

barco

firetruck

camión de bomberos

train

tren

toys

juguetes

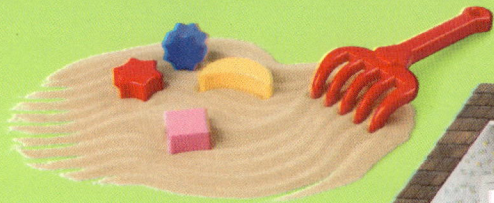

Printed in Great Britain
by Amazon

21746756R00025